9/92

D0408550

MENTAL RETARDATION

MENTAL RETARDATION

by Robert E. Dunbar

A Venture Book
Franklin Watts
New York/London/Toronto/Sydney
1991

For Chaz and other counselors and case
managers whose compassionate guidance is
helping persons with mental retardation
to achieve higher levels of independence
and self-respect

Photographs copyright ©: Photo Researchers, Inc.: 14 (Catherine Ursillo), 22,
45 (both Bruce Roberts), 64 top (Van Bucher), 71 (Robert Goldstein);
Springer/Bettmann Film Archive: p. 27; Perkins School for the Blind: p. 29;
The Bettmann Archive: p. 32; Monkmeyer Press Photo: pp. 39 (Freda
Leinwand), 73 (MacPherson); Stock Boston, Inc.: pp. 41 (Bohdan
Hrynewych), 52 (Lionel Delevingne), 54 (Pamela Price), 64 bottom (Michael
Hayman), 65 (Elizabeth Crews).

Library of Congress Cataloging-in-Publication Data

Dunbar, Robert E.
Mental retardation / by Robert E. Dunbar.
p.   cm. — (A Venture book)
Includes bibliographical references and index.
Summary: Examines the causes, health problems, and prevention of
mental retardation and discusses education and research involving
the mentally retarded.
ISBN 0-531-12502-5
1. Mentally handicapped—United States—Juvenile literature.
2. Mental retardation—Juvenile literature.   [1. Mental
retardation.   2. Mentally handicapped.]   I. Title. II. Series.
HV3006.A4D86   1991
362.3'0973—dc20   91-18513 CIP AC

Contents

1
Myths and Facts

If you have never had any experience with a mentally retarded child or adult, your conceptions about the disabilities common to this condition are probably based on myths. For instance, you might think that persons with mental retardation are unable to learn even the simplest tasks and certainly are unable to attend school. You might picture in your mind people who speak gibberish and who always act childishly. You might picture people who frequently have to be restrained to prevent them from accidentally harming themselves or others. You might think that persons with mental retardation are completely helpless and hopeless and should be either hidden away at home or put in an institution with the mentally ill. If you think any of these things, you are wrong.

DEFINING MENTAL RETARDATION

The American Association on Mental Retardation (AAMR) is an organization that has striven for decades to destroy the myths about mental retardation and provide a definition of this disability based on scientific fact and experience. In 1990 the AAMR comprehensive definition that addressed the two salient aspects of measuring a person's competence: intelligence and adaptive ability. According to the AAMR, a person with mental retardation is below average in his or her ability to learn. Also, a person with mental retardation will have difficulty in learning some, but not necessarily all, adaptive skills.[1]

This will depend on several factors, including the person's degree of mental retardation as measured by standard Intelligence Quotient (IQ) tests as well as the cultural environment. Listed under adaptive skills are: communication, self-care, social skills, functional academics, practical skills, leisure, use of the community, self-direction, work, and independent living. The AAMR has also stated that mental retardation begins prior to age eighteen but may not always be of lifelong duration.

Unless you have grown up with a brother or sister with mental retardation, it may be difficult at first to understand the problems this can create within a family. It can be a painfully disruptive experience unless the actions of all members of the family are ruled by a positive attitude. How do you think you would respond if you had a brother or sister who was born with mental retardation? The account that follows shows how a brother and his parents were able to adapt to this situation in a positive way.

JOEY'S STORY

When Joey was born he had a hematoma, or localized swelling filled with blood, on his brain.[2] The resulting brain damage caused his mental retardation. As is often the case with children born with mental retardation, however, there were other disabilities as well, although in Joey's case they didn't show up until later. Joey was born with epilepsy, a nervous disorder in which there are recurring attacks of motor, sensory, or psychic malfunctions. The attacks can occur with or without unconsciousness or convulsive movements and are known as seizures. It wasn't until Joey was eleven years old that he had his first seizure.

Joey had another serious illness, poliomyelitis (sometimes called polio or infantile paralysis), when he was five years old. An infectious disease caused by a virus that attacks the central nervous system, polio can result in paralysis, muscular atrophy, and often deformity. Joey was paralyzed on both sides of his body and lost his fine motor skills. It took several years for him to recover. He is only bothered slightly on one side of his body now. Several years after Joey had polio, a vaccine was developed to protect children and adults from this disease.

Joey and His Brother

It was during the time Joey developed polio that his brother Richard was born. As a youngster, Richard was not aware of what it meant for a person to be born with mental retardation, and no incidents stand out in his early years. Joey has only a mild degree of mental retardation when measured by IQ tests, and that may be one reason why Richard was not aware of his brother's disability in his early years.

When Richard entered his teen years, however, he began to realize that his older brother Joey "wasn't like I was," and began to understand what it meant to be a person with mental retardation. He also began to feel the need to protect his brother, an attitude that his parents encouraged. As Richard recalls, his parents always had a very caring attitude where Joey was concerned and always did whatever they could to help him and encourage him to live as independently as possible. Whatever disappointment his parents may have felt when Joey was born was never apparent to Richard. He remembers only a caring attitude and constant efforts to help him learn life skills. They were willing to accept the fact that Joey had been born with mental retardation and adjust their lives accordingly.

The care and responsibility of a child with mental retardation, however, probably affected their plans for having more children. Richard was the only child born after Joey. The parents' concern and sense of responsibility carried over to Richard, especially as he became older. Richard recalled that Joey's epilepsy was always troublesome. His seizures were frightening and made Richard want to do what he could to protect his brother. Once he took Joey with him when he went fishing on a nearby lake. Everything was fine until Joey either lost his balance or had a seizure and fell out of the boat. Richard recalled, "I immediately threw out two life preservers and jumped in to save him. I just barely made it back to the boat in time."

Attending Public Schools

Richard doesn't recall any special educational programs for children with mental retardation when Joey was growing up, but apparently there were no serious problems when Joey attended the local public schools. He was passed on from grade to grade, staying with children in his age group until he reached his freshman year in high school, when he had to drop out of school because of learning difficulties and other adjustment problems.

His parents knew that Joey could benefit from continued education and training, especially if he was going to be able to attain a certain level of independence. This was something they deeply desired for his sake, especially for the time when they would no longer be there to care for him. With this in mind, Joey was sent out of state to a private school for children with mental retardation. However, he soon became homesick and returned home. Not much could be done to help him at that time, either in his home state or in the local community. It was not until 1978 that a local private agency for adults with mental retardation was organized. Since then, Joey has continued to receive counseling and training. It is also the source of his part-time job. He works from two to four hours a day as custodian at the Activity Center.

When his father died, Joey continued to live at home with his mother, his brother Richard, and Richard's wife. Theirs is a large house in a small town that would be considered rural by today's standards, although farming is no longer a major occupation in the area. Living in a small town rather than in a city has advantages for Joey. His family knows that if anything should happen to him, a seizure or some other calamity, someone in the community would notify them immediately. Richard calls it "a caring community," and he and his mother are grateful for that.

His Own Apartment

The fact that his parents always encouraged him to be as independent as possible has helped Joey to cope better than some other persons with mental retardation. The family home is spacious enough for Joey to have his own "apartment," separate from the rest of the house. His living space includes a kitchen with stove, refrigerator, and dishwasher, and a bedroom/sitting room. He can do many things for himself, including cooking and keeping his apartment clean and in good order. His mother and brother are able to keep fairly close watch over him. They doubt if he could live completely on his own outside the family home. For example, he needs to take medicine for his epilepsy, so Richard checks from time to time to make sure he has taken the medication. Also, he takes Joey to the doctor for periodic checkups. This kind of assistance, however, is now available through home health care agencies and by public social workers.

Richard helps Joey shop for food, clothes, and other items. Because of his disability Joey receives Social Security payments from the federal government, and this money, plus what he earns from part-time jobs, is used for his rent, heat, food, and other necessities. He does not handle this money on his own. Every two weeks he is given fifty dollars to buy food. He makes out his own shopping list, and then he and his brother go shopping together. Joey can cook, but he doesn't like to go to a lot of trouble, so he tends to buy prepared foods such as ready-made dinners. His brother also goes with him when he buys clothes, encouraging him to choose what he wants and to be aware of how much clothes and accessory items cost.

Awareness of Opposite Sex

According to his brother, Joey is aware of the opposite sex and wonders from time to time what it might be like to have a girlfriend or to get married. He has a certain amount of social interaction with women who are mentally retarded at the local Activity Center, but he has never had the opportunity to "date" in the usual sense of the word. Although he has stirrings from time to time, he has never had a strong urge in this direction.

Compared to other men and women who are only mildly retarded, Joey has a relatively good life and has benefited from the programs offered by the local agency for adults with mental retardation. His family, however, would like to see more funding for private and public agencies so they could offer more programs and pay better salaries to keep the best qualified professionals on their staff. Too often good case managers and counselors are lost when attracted by better-paying jobs.

HOW OTHER FAMILIES COPE

When a child is born with mental retardation, the immediate problem may be to meet the needs of the parents in their grief, disappointment, and other complex emotional responses.[3] How well they learn to adjust to this event will affect not only the child but themselves and the child's brothers and sisters. This is especially true in families in which the birth of a child with mental retardation is either rare or unknown.

Any negative reactions and feelings take their toll on all family members until they learn to accept the child and provide the love and care that is needed. One positive development in recent years is that prospects have improved markedly for many children with mental retardation. Eventually, through education and training, many can become self-sufficient enough to live independently in the community, with limited supervision. With this in mind, parents of a child with mental retardation are cautioned against being too protective or not encouraging the child to learn and progress at whatever rate he or she may be capable of. Too much protectiveness can result in understimulation of the child and lost learning opportunities.

A child with mental retardation, by definition, learns more slowly and will need special, sustained instruction to learn self-help and other life skills. A child with mental retardation must have positive reinforcement to make this possible. This is an important role for parents, who must learn how to encourage their child. Their energies need to be channeled in positive directions, focusing attention on the child's full potential rather than on his or her disabilities. For most parents, this is not easy to achieve without counseling. At the same time they need to be realistic and not fall prey to gross overexpectations. In viewing the child's progress, parents should compare it against the child's earlier performance and not against the progress of children who do not have this disability.

Response of
Brothers and Sisters

When a child with mental retardation has brothers and sisters, problems of acceptance may develop as they grow older. Much will depend on the attitude of the parents. If the parents find their child a source of anxiety and embarrassment, so will the child's sisters and brothers. They may

In raising a child with mental retardation, parents and other caregivers should focus on the child's full potential, rather than on the youngster's disability.

prefer not to bring friends home and tend to play elsewhere. On the other hand, a loving, caring attitude on the parents' part can be passed on to the child's sisters and brothers. This is the kind of positive reinforcement that a child with mental retardation needs.

A professional in the mental retardation field once reported the pride and relief of a devoted mother of a five-year-old boy with mental retardation when her eight-year-old son promised her that he would take care of his little brother when he grew up. Like all parents of children who are mentally retarded, there is deep concern about what might happen to their child when they die. For this and other reasons it is important for parents as well as brothers and sisters to encourage the child with mental retardation to learn how to be as independent as possible. The trend in empowerment and education is to help mentally retarded children and adults to achieve that goal.

The need for goals becomes apparent when parents are asked, "What if your child was left alone in the house for twenty-four hours? Could she keep warm, keep the doors locked, use the telephone, bathe or wash safely?" Whether these skills—and goals—are possible will depend on the degree of mental retardation and how well the child responds to education and training. Many children with mental retardation are capable of learning how to take care of their personal needs and help with domestic chores, if the lessons are carefully taught and practiced regularly.

Behavior Problems at Home

If a child's parents are uninformed or uncooperative, this can lead to serious behavior problems, especially at home. The case of Tom, a fifteen-year-old boy with mental retardation, is a good example. At school his behavior was unexceptional, but at home he would grossly overeat and made no effort to control his bowels. He often created scenes in which he would lie on the sidewalk or scream in the car if he was thwarted in any way. When he was taken

15

out of the home for assessment, it was found that because of his height and weight, he was very difficult to manage and had become physically aggressive toward his parents. He lacked many basic skills, such as the ability to wash and dress himself or to clear a meal from the table.

Part of the problem was that he had a very poor image of himself and was obsessed with his fecal functioning. When he was started on various "goal plans," he began to respond well because of the encouragement and praise he received as he began to make progress. He learned to bathe and dress himself and to perform certain domestic chores. When controls were put on his diet, his bowels began to function normally, and he became thinner and more personally attractive.

Tom's case is an example of an adolescent with mental retardation who was spoiled and overprotected at home by uninformed and indulgent parents. Many parents tend to give up too soon, without finding out how much their child can be helped in achieving life skills and a certain level of independence.

2
Causes of
Mental Retardation

According to the American Association on Mental Retardation (AAMR), there are at least 350 known causes of mental retardation, "but this list is almost certainly incomplete."[1] Among the known causes are (1) genetic disorders in which a single gene is involved; (2) genetic disorders caused by the interaction of several genes; and (3) chromosome disorders in which abnormalities result from errors that occur during the formation of either the sperm in the male or the egg in the female.

The nucleus of every human cell contains a substance known as DNA (deoxyribonucleic acid), which contains all of a person's genetic material. In other words, DNA contains the genes that determine such inherited characteristics as hair color, body shape and height, skin color, shape of hands and legs, eye color and shape, as well as a tendency toward certain diseases. The genetic material in each cell is organized into subunits called *chromosomes*. In a normal human being, there are twenty-three pairs of chromosomes. In each pair, one chromosome comes from the

17

mother and one from the father. However, there are sex differences. A female child will have two X chromosomes, one from each parent; but a male child will have an X chromosome from his mother and a Y chromosome from his father.[2]

RECESSIVE AND DOMINANT GENES

A gene may mutate (change) or become abnormal as a result of some change in the DNA structure. Whether or not this causes a problem depends on the kind of gene created—a recessive (weak) gene or a dominant (strong) gene. When a recessive gene is paired with a dominant gene, the dominant gene will prevail. This may not cause any problems unless the dominant gene happens to be abnormal. Problems can also result when both genes in a pair are recessive and abnormal. Sometimes these problems show up at birth and sometimes not until much later, when the affected person is an adult.

One example of a health problem caused by an abnormal dominant gene is *Von Recklinghausen's disease.* This disease occurs once in every 3,000 births and is marked by a skin lesion known as café-au-lait (coffee-with-milk) spots. These are irregular, oval-shaped patches of light brown color. Physical problems associated with this disease include scoliosis or curvature of the spine, a larger than normal head, and the formation of nodules both on and under the skin, which can be quite disfiguring. About 12 percent of persons born with this disease have seizures and about 10 percent are mentally retarded.

A disease caused by an abnormal dominant gene that usually occurs when the affected person is an adult is *myotonic dystrophy*, a common type of muscular dystrophy. This disease may appear any time from infancy to old age, but it usually affects a person when he or she is in her late twenties. Persons with this disease have difficulty in relaxing contracted muscles, especially muscles in the jaw and hands. The facial appearance is marked by a drooping mouth and eyelids. In addition to nerves and muscles, many other organ systems may be affected. This disease is also marked by varying degrees of mental retardation.

X-LINKED RECESSIVE DISORDERS

When the problem is an *X-linked recessive disorder*, the abnormal gene is located on the X chromosome. Only males are affected because they have only one X chromosome, which comes from the mother. This is paired with a Y chromosome, which comes from the father. This abnormality is inherited from the mother. A well-known example of an X-linked recessive disorder is *Lesch-Nyhan syndrome*, which is an inherited form of cerebral palsy. Along with the spasticity associated with this disease, there is also mental retardation and a compulsion for self-mutilation.

Male children born with this disease usually appear normal at birth and for the first few months of infancy. Often the first sign of the disease is the discovery of an orange, sandlike substance in the baby's diapers. These are uric acid crystals, caused by an inborn error of purine metabolism in which the child's body produces excessive amounts of uric acid. Affected infants soon lose the ability to sit independently and begin to show signs of cerebral palsy, with its spasticity and compulsive movements. Most persons with Lesch-Nyhan syndrome are moderately retarded, attaining an IQ that is usually less than 50. Eventually they are able to develop some speech.

There are often severe medical complications as well as behavior problems that are difficult to manage. Persons with Lesch-Nyhan syndrome tend to bite their lips and fingers so severely that it often results in tissue damage and loss. Also, they are aggressive toward other children. Many have to be physically restrained in order to protect them from themselves as well as to protect other children.

NEURAL TUBE DEFECTS

Although a significant proportion of mental retardation may be caused by single gene disorders, the largest proportion by far involves the interaction of several defective genes, complicated by other factors. This category includes *neural tube defects*. Three examples of this birth defect are (1) anencephaly, a severe and fatal defect in the development of the brain; (2) encephalocele, in which brain tissue protrudes through a defect in the cranium; and (3) spina bifida, in which part of the bony spine that helps protect the spinal cord fails to develop. As a result of this the nerves of the spinal cord in that area are exposed and unprotected and may also be defective.

Neural tube defects in the United States are fairly common, occurring in about one in 500 births. The survival rate is about 90 percent. Most children born with neural tube defects develop hydrocephalus. This is an accumulation of fluid in the brain, causing an enlargement of the head. This condition has been treated successfully by the surgical insertion of a shunt to help drain excess fluid from the brain. Neural tube defects often cause mental retardation as well as problems of bladder and bowel incontinence.

DOWN SYNDROME

Another common cause of mental retardation is a disorder in the arrangement of chromosomes.[3] This can involve the translocation of chromosomes, that is, chromosomes found in the wrong place, or chromosomes that are either missing parts or that have too many parts. One of the best-known examples of mental retardation caused by a chromosome disorder is *Down syndrome*. A child with Down syndrome is usually shorter than normal, has a small head and ears, and slanted eyes. A small nose and a depressed nasal bridge give the impression of a face that is flatter than normal.

The neck is usually short and broad. The tongue is fissured, and teeth take longer to erupt and are often abnormally shaped. There may also be abnormalities of fingers and toes. About 40 percent of children with Down syndrome have congenital heart disease, and a large percentage have umbilical hernias.

In the first few months of life a child with Down syndrome will be more like normal infants and follow a similar sequence of development. However, the child's physical and psychomotor development is usually delayed, and so is the ability to speak. Studies have shown a wide variation in mental abilities among children with Down syndrome.

With appropriate care, most Down syndrome children will be functioning in the mild to moderate range of mental retardation. Supportive counseling of parents, good home care, early intervention, and environmental enrichment are some of the factors that will make this possible. Others include stimulating preschool experiences and, while in school, special education. As with other children with varying degrees of mental retardation, even those with the most challenging cognitive and physical disabilities, Down syndrome children have the potential to become productive citizens when given appropriate life-skills training and supports.[4]

Several chromosome disorders have been shown to be associated with Down syndrome, but by far the most common is trisomy 21, in which chromosome 21 has three chromosomes instead of the normal two. This is the case in about 95 percent of children with Down syndrome. The risk of having a child with Down syndrome has been shown to increase with the age of the parents, especially the mother. While the age of the father has been shown to be the determining factor in about 25 percent of cases of trisomy 21 disorder, about 75 percent have been shown to be caused by the mother's age at the time of conception.

A great deal of progress has been made in recent years in identifying many different kinds of chromosome disor-

21

Those affected with Down syndrome usually have a smaller head and ears, a flat nose, and slanted eyes. Most suffer from mild or moderate mental retardation, but with proper education and support, can function as productive citizens.

ders that may cause a child to be born with mental retardation. The risk of some disorders is slight, but for others the risk is much greater. For this reason chromosome disorders are among the factors considered when prospective parents seek the benefits of genetic counseling before they decide to have a child.

HEALTH HAZARDS BEFORE
AND DURING BIRTH

Every mother-to-be hopes for a relatively easy birth when her child is born, but there is much more at stake than an easy delivery. The baby's health—from the time it is conceived through all the weeks and months that it is in the mother's womb—is crucial, and can be threatened unless precautions are taken. For example, the fetus's blood circulation and the amount of oxygen in the blood are vitally important. Poor circulation and a lack of oxygen are some of the factors that can cause a child to be born mentally retarded. Below-normal flow of blood to and from the brain can cause brain damage; brain cells die when they do not receive enough blood or oxygen.

One of the earliest tests of the health of newborn babies is the *Apgar score*, based on a three-point scale given to five different birth conditions: heart rate, cry, muscle tone, color, and reflexes. The predictive value of the one-minute Apgar score has been questioned, but the extended score after five minutes has been shown to be a good indicator of the likelihood of cerebral palsy. Many who score poorly will be mentally retarded.

INFECTIONS OF
MOTHER AND CHILD

Infections in the brain area account for a significant number of children who are born with mental retardation. Infection can occur while the child is in its mother's uterus, or womb, or when the child is born. Those that occur in the mother's uterus have a destructive effect on nervous tissue and interfere with the development of the brain. The most frequent and serious threat is caused by *cytomegalovirus* (CMV) infection. CMV infection causes an inflammation of brain tissue and the membrane that covers the brain. This can result in destruction of brain tissue and cause various malformations, such as microcephaly, or a smaller head than normal. It can also cause enlargement of the liver and spleen, a generalized skin rash, a low platelet count, and seizures.

Another serious infection is *rubella*, or German measles. If a pregnant woman contracts this disease, it can cause defects in the child's eyes, ears, and heart. Rubella interferes with the growth of cells in the developing brain and may cause inflammation and destruction of tissues. Another complication that contributes to destruction of brain cells is an inflammation of the walls of blood vessels. In addition to mental retardation, children affected by this disease are often born with cataracts and other eye problems as well as hearing loss. Other consequences may include a narrowing of the pulmonary artery, which interferes with heart function. Immunizing children with the rubella vaccine can help prevent the spread of this virus in the general population, including pregnant women. Immunization of susceptible pregnant women (who have not had the disease before and become immune) is another major method of preventing this disease.

SEXUALLY TRANSMITTED DISEASES

Any infection in a pregnant woman can have serious consequences for the child she is bearing, either while it is in the womb or during birth. Among the serious infections that can affect a child when it is born and result in mental retardation are the sexually transmitted diseases. An example of this is the *herpes simplex virus*. When active in the mother's vagina, out of sight and unknown to the mother or her doctor, this virus can cause meningoencephalitis, or inflammation of the membranes that enclose the newborn child's brain and spinal cord. This infection is acquired in one of two ways. One is when birth begins with the rupture of the fetal-maternal membranes, allowing the virus to ascend into the birth canal. The other is when the newborn child passes through the mother's birth canal. This infection can be fatal or it may be localized in the central nervous system, eyes, skin, or mouth. In the case of herpes simplex type 2, when it is severe it can cause massive hemorrhage and swelling in the brain and destruction of brain tissue.

Another sexually transmitted disease that can result in mental retardation is *congenital syphilis*. This dread disease had been declining to vanishing low levels with the advent of antibiotics, but it has recently been on the rise again. The mother may be entirely without symptoms that would warn her or her doctor of the presence of infection. In that case it could only be detected by means of a blood test. When congenital syphilis affects the nervous system it causes meningitis, or inflammation of the membranes enclosing the brain and spinal cord, and may lead to hydrocephalus, or the accumulation of fluid in the brain.

3
Opportunities for Education and Training

Concern for the education and training of persons with mental retardation has a long history that stretches back to the late eighteenth century in Europe. One of the early leaders was the French physician Jean-Marc Itard. In 1800 Itard was summoned for consultation when a twelve-year-old boy named Victor was found living wild in Aveyron Forest in southern France. The boy had evidently been abandoned by his parents. When Dr. Itard examined him, he found that the boy had mental retardation. His animal-like behavior, however, was not due to his retardation but was the result of his isolation and lack of human stimulation. With Dr. Itard's help, Victor eventually was able to learn language and self-help skills. Dr. Itard also tried to teach him social skills, with the ultimate goal of making him more socially compatible. This continues to be one of the primary objectives of workers in the mental retardation field: helping those with mental retardation to achieve more independence and self-respect.

Another important step was taken by a student of Dr. Itard, Edward O. Séguin, who established the first public

In 1800, Victor, a mentally retarded twelve-year-old, was found living wild in a forest in southern France. Through the efforts of Dr. Jean-Marc Itard, he was able to learn language and other important life skills. This is a still from a movie based on Victor's story entitled The Wild Child.

residential facility for children with moderate mental retardation. As part of his education and training efforts, Seguin concentrated on ways in which children with mental retardation could develop motor and sensory skills and improve the functioning of their nervous systems.

At about the same time an American, Samuel Gridley Howe, introduced Seguin's teaching methods in the first state residential facility for the mentally retarded in the United States. This milestone was reached in 1848, when he was granted funds from the Massachusetts legislature to create a residential school for ten children with mental retardation. Before then, children with mental retardation either stayed at home or were sent to charity institutions or poorhouses. In 1850, a survey showed that 60 percent of the residents in poorhouses had some degree of mental retardation.

In the decades that followed, many residential schools for children with mental retardation were established as well as asylums for the mentally ill. In fact, at that time persons with mental retardation and the mentally ill were lumped together in the public view and received the same type of services. However, facilities for persons with mental retardation were often located in rural areas where agricultural work was available. Those who were able to work on nearby farms were able to contribute to the cost of some of their expenses. Being located in a rural area, however, meant that they were more isolated from the community of normal citizens than they would have been if they had been housed in heavily populated areas.

The beginning decades of the twentieth century saw an increase in the subsidy and sponsorship of public schools to benefit children with mental retardation. In 1950 the National Association for Retarded Children was established with the chief goal of developing public school programs for mentally retarded children. Eleven years later, in 1961, President John F. Kennedy's first panel on mental retardation promoted legislation that would enforce the rights

*Samuel Gridley Howe (1801–1876) built
the first residential school for mentally
retarded children in the United States.*

of persons with mental retardation to education and other social services. These trends were further strengthened in 1966, when the Bureau for the Handicapped was established as part of the Department of Health, Education, and Welfare. This made more services available to children and adults with mental retardation.

A MORE NORMAL COMMUNITY SETTING

It was not until the 1970s that a strong movement was created to place persons with mental retardation in a more normal community setting, and to provide services for all handicapped children, no matter how severely handicapped they might be.[1] This movement developed in response to evidence that children with mental retardation who could be educated were more likely to show improvement if they were placed in regular rather than special classes. There was also legal pressure from minority groups who contended that disadvantaged minority children were being mislabeled as retarded and inappropriately placed in special education programs.

These and other pressures led to the landmark legislation of 1975, *Public Law 94-142*, which was designed to guarantee that all citizens with disabilities, including those with mental retardation, would receive appropriate education from age three to age twenty-one. This law states that the education must be individualized for the child. Also, all students with disabilities must be integrated, or mainstreamed, into regular education programs "to the maximum extent possible."

CLASSIFYING THOSE WITH MENTAL RETARDATION

Among the major factors considered when classifying a child as mentally retarded are intelligence and behavior, in particular adaptive behavior.[2] A school-age child who performs below average on an intelligence test but still manages to succeed in the regular classroom, if only on a marginal level, would not be classified as having mental retardation. In this case it is assumed that the child's adaptive behavior reflects a higher level of intellect than is indicated by the intelligence test. Another exception would be the child who is not able to adapt to the regular classroom but whose intelligence test score indicates normal intelligence. The child's inability to adapt to the regular classroom in this case might be the result of emotional problems rather than limited intelligence.

Children with mental retardation are usually classified according to their level of intelligence, based on standard IQ tests. Those who are mildly to moderately retarded have an IQ range of 75 to 50. The IQs of those who are severely or profoundly retarded range from 50 to 30 or less. In times past there used to be a classification for the "borderline or slow learner," those with an IQ that ranged from 70 to 85, but this classification is no longer considered valid.

ORIGIN AND DEVELOPMENT
OF INTELLIGENCE TESTS

The French psychologist Alfred Binet is considered the outstanding pioneer in the development of the modern intelligence test.[3] It was Binet and his student, Theodore Simon, who in the early years of the twentieth century began to work on a test that would identify mental retardation among French schoolchildren. In 1905 this resulted in the *Binet-Simon Intelligence Scale*. It contained problems designed to measure memory, reasoning ability, the ability to compare objects, numerical skills, comprehension, time orientation, the ability to combine ideas into meaningful wholes, and knowledge of common objects and ideas. Binet continued to work on intelligence tests until his death in 1911, making three major innovations in mental testing.

31

Alfred Binet (1857–1911), shocked by the treatment of the mentally retarded in France, developed an intelligence test that would determine which children required specialized education.

According to American psychologist Lewis M. Terman, Binet was the first to use age standards in measuring intelligence. Under his method, a test was considered to measure mental ability at a specific age if two-thirds to three-quarters of children of that age could pass it. Secondly, Binet measured the higher and more complex mental processes in contrast to the more elemental processes that had been used in previous tests.

Binet also conceived intelligence as the sum of all thought processes in mental adaptation, emphasizing three characteristics: (1) the tendency to take and maintain a definite direction; (2) the capacity to adapt in order to attain a goal; and (3) the power of self-criticism. Binet was also careful to include a test problem only if the percentage of those able to solve it increased with the age of the person being tested and only if children known to be bright solved it more frequently than those known to be dull.

Binet's work was later refined by Terman, who in 1916 published the Stanford Revision of the Binet-Simon Test, which later became known as the *Stanford-Binet Intelligence Test*. This test dominated the field of mental testing for more than twenty years. After undergoing revisions, it is still in use today. Another American psychologist, David Wechsler, designed the Wechsler-Bellvue Intelligence Scale, for use with adults, in 1939, and the *Wechsler Intelligence Scale for Children*, ten years later. In 1955, he revised his test for adults, producing the *Wechsler Adult Intelligence Scale*. The Wechsler tests provide three distinct IQs (intelligence quotients), one for the entire test, one for the group of verbal tests, and the third for the performance tests. When evaluated by an experienced expert, the test is supposed to be able to reveal insights concerning emotional problems of those being tested.

Another contributor to developments in intelligence testing was Arthur S. Otis, who had studied with Terman. In 1916 he created the *Otis Group Test of Mental Ability*, which was the first intelligence test that did not have to be administered to only one subject at a time. Later this led to the development of the Otis Group Intelligence Scale and the Otis Self-Administering Test of Mental Ability, which measures a wide variety of skills. Whichever test is used, however, it should be stressed that a person's IQ scores tend to change throughout life and are not always accurate indicators of intelligence. According to some researchers in the field of intelligence, IQ scores at times reflect both cultural and economic bias.

EDUCATING CHILDREN WITH
MENTAL RETARDATION

According to the American Association on Mental Retardation, even though a child with mental retardation may not be able to benefit sufficiently from regular classes, he or she is still considered to have learning potential in three areas. One is academic—the ability to learn at the primary or advanced elementary grade level. The second is social— the ability to learn social skills and to be able to get along independently in the community. The third is vocational— the ability to learn work skills in order to be either partially or totally self-supporting as an adult.

Some children are not identified as retarded until they enter school and begin to exhibit learning disabilities. One reason for this is that some parents are not as concerned as others about their child's intellectual development. They are not disturbed by the child being slow in learning how to talk or showing poor motor skills. They may believe the child will eventually outgrow these deficiencies. However, when the child is unable to keep up with children of normal intelligence and shows other disabilities associated with mental retardation, it soon becomes obvious to parents as well as teachers and school officials that the child has mental retardation and needs special help.

The kind of help given will include training in good study habits, how to follow directions, and special training in reading and math. Once this groundwork is laid, the child with mental retardation can begin learning other subjects, including spelling and writing. Study of these and other basic subjects will continue through adolescence.

In later years the emphasis will be on preparing for work and independent home living. One of the most important objectives, and one that is difficult for some children with mental retardation to attain, is to develop a sense of personal adequacy. If a child with mental retardation is frequently frustrated and overcome by a sense of failure, his or her emotional well-being is threatened. It is further threatened unless the child can feel a sense of belonging to the class and is able to form friendships with his classmates.

POTENTIAL FOR LEARNING

Sometimes the potential for learning among children with varying degrees of mental retardation may depend more on environmental and educational opportunities than IQ level. However, the problems exhibited by children with severe or profound mental retardation show up quite early in the preschool years. Many of these children have multiple disabilities. Generally speaking, they have the potential for learning self-help skills; social adjustment in the family and neighborhood; and economic usefulness in the home, in a residential school, or in a supported employment program.

Opportunities for training are available as early as age three in many communities, often in a special day schools organized for this purpose. Here they are given training in dressing, feeding, and toileting. The emphasis is on oral language development, self-help skills, socialization, and, in later school years, on preparation for living and working with supervision. They receive practice in the following skills:

- listening
- following directions

- communicating with others
- reading and recognizing commonly encountered signs and labels
- counting
- telling time

They also receive lessons in dressing, grooming, eating, care of personal belongings, good toileting hygiene, and safety. They are encouraged to participate in arts and crafts, sports, and other forms of recreation according to their abilities. As they reach adolescence they begin vocational training and practice in home-living skills. With the help of other professionals, such as public health nurses who visit the home and provide guidance in child care and management, parents are sometimes able to maintain the child at home throughout his or her school years.

THE CHILD WITH SEVERE
MENTAL RETARDATION

It is only in recent years that the child with severe mental retardation has been able to benefit from special education programs. One reason for this is that in the past, in order to be eligible, a child had to be toilet-trained and be able to communicate. Oftentimes the only care those with severe mental retardation received was in private or public institutions. However, legislation now requires educational classification systems to include those persons with severe and profound mental retardation. These children can learn certain life skills but their capabilities are limited. They are taught toileting, self-dressing, and self-feeding, but even these tasks are beyond some children. Those persons with severe mental retardation have a much more limited potential to achieve some degree of independence as adults. They will need fairly constant supervision throughout their lives under supported employment and supported living programs.

A MORE
STRUCTURED APPROACH

Because their comprehension level is low and they learn slowly, children with mental retardation, whether in private or public schools, need a much more carefully structured approach than regular students do. This same approach is needed when they are involved in physical education and vocational development classes. A student's physical disabilities must also be considered. Awkwardness, clumsiness, slow reactions, and confusion are common problems that take time and patience to correct or overcome. Those who are mildly retarded often have vision, hearing, and neurological problems. The greater the degree of retardation, the more likely that the child's disabilities will be greater. As in all groups of students, however, there will be a range of learning abilities, depending on the degree of intelligence and the child's success in adaptive behavior. Periodic evaluation is needed in order to make appropriate adjustments in each child's educational and other programs.

SPECIAL PROGRAMS VS.
REGULAR CLASSROOM INSTRUCTION

Many studies have been conducted on how students with mental retardation respond to special education programs vs. regular instruction in the classroom, with varying results. Some individuals need special programs in order to make progress in their learning efforts. Others are able to benefit from instruction in a regular classroom with relatively little assistance. Studies have also shown that when a mentally retarded child in regular classes is rejected by his peers, it is usually not because of his low intelligence but because there are behavior problems that need to be resolved.

The trend is to place students with mental retardation

in regular classrooms whenever possible, even in the case of children who need special help. This is in line with the concept of "least restrictive environment" that was mandated by Public Law 94-142. It was this law that led to the parallel concept of mainstreaming children with mental retardation in public schools. This concept has the following features:

1. The mainstreamed child must spend more than half his or her time in the regular classroom.
2. The regular classroom teacher must have primary responsibility for the child's progress.
3. No categorical labels, such as mentally retarded or emotionally disturbed, must be applied to the child.
4. The child's disabilities must not be so severe as to inhibit his ability to learn in a regular classroom setting.

The Resource Room was a direct outgrowth of the mainstreaming concept. Here special assistance is given by teachers trained to work with mentally retarded students as well as with students who have learning difficulties in one or more subjects. The Resource Room has certain advantages over special classrooms. For one thing, students do not have to be labeled as slow learners or mentally retarded in order to get this kind of help, and they can continue to be with their classmates for part of the school day. The Resource Room also makes it possible for more students to be served for a limited number of hours than would be the case in an all-day special classroom, which makes it cost-effective.

In spite of the advantages that mainstreaming offers children who are mentally retarded, the concept has not been fully accepted by all educators. One of the overriding concerns is when and how it is best accomplished. Before

Mainstreaming provides mentally retarded children with the opportunity to make progress in a regular classroom environment and to learn appropriate social behavior. The child on the right has Down syndrome.

accepting a child with mental retardation in a regular classroom, the following factors are usually considered: (1) changes required in the classroom in order to accommodate the child; (2) the child's social skills and relationships with his peers; (3) the teacher's attitude about mainstreaming and ability to cope with a mentally retarded child; and (4) the attitude of the child's family and what kind of support system is in place.

RESIDENTIAL SCHOOLS AND INSTITUTIONS

Another way of providing care and training for a child with mental retardation, depending on the circumstances, is to place the child in a residential school or institution. These facilities range from hospitals that provide primarily medical treatment for children with severe to profound mental retardation and other major disabilities to residential schools with educational programs for children whose primary needs do not include medical attention. A residential school or institution is often the last resort for children whose needs cannot be met in public schools.

The major advantage from a treatment point of view is that these schools or institutions are able to provide medical, psychological, social welfare, and educational services for a large number of children with similar disabilities at one location. However, there are disadvantages. First, the child is removed from home and is therefore cut off from association with parents, brothers, and sisters. The child is also denied the opportunity for informal and spontaneous contact with nonretarded children of a similar age. Another disadvantage is that there is a stigma attached to the residents. Whatever the degree of retardation, to be so labeled is harmful when it suggests automatically that the child or adult can expect a life of dependency, helplessness, and hopelessness.

Residential facilities provide education and medical treatment to mentally retarded youngsters whose needs cannot be met in public schools.

FROM ISOLATION
TO INTEGRATION

Prospects for more humane treatment and better educational and vocational opportunities have improved considerably for the child with mental retardation. One hopeful development came in 1986, when the U.S. Congress added a new section to the Education of the Handicapped Act, providing funds for early intervention services in each state. One direct result was the implementation of approaches in meeting the needs of infants and toddlers with mental retardation. Getting the help they need at an early age considerably improves their prospects for learning important life skills and for achieving a measure of independence in their adult years.[4]

Also in 1986, the Rehabilitation Act was revised to provide funding for vocational training for individuals with severe disabilities, which includes those with mental retardation. This training extends to supported employment, an on-the-job training approach that places a coach at the job site for as long as is needed for the individual to develop the skills needed to perform the task. Commented one mental retardation professional, "Where states have been successful in funding supported employment, it has been a resounding success. There are supported employment programs in each state, and the systems are developing and growing rapidly."

4
Improving the Quality
of Life

As recently as a generation ago the attitude shared by many parents of mentally retarded children, especially those in the severely or profoundly retarded range, was that the children would be better off placed in an institution where they could receive constant professional care. Major reasons for this attitude were the frustration experienced by parents who did not know how to help their children and the absence of community agencies that could provide the help and direction needed. The trend is now toward de-institutionalization of children and adults with mental retardation, with education and training provided so they can live in the community or in public or private community residences with minimum supervision.

For those children who were placed in institutions but are now considered good candidates for some kind of community living arrangement, the transition can be difficult or impossible without parental support. This was emphasized in an account given by Thomas K. Gilhool of the testimony of a seventy-seven-year-old woman, Grace Auerbach, whose son, Sidney, had been placed in an institution called Pennhurst in the mid-1930s. Gilhool wrote in 1980: "He left Pennhurst about 1975 and has since lived first in a group home and now in a supervised apartment with two retarded friends. According to his mother, while at Pennhurst Sidney was subdued and never talked. Now he is always ready to engage in conversation. He is employed and has his own bank account.

"Sidney has learned more in the last three and a half years while in the community than he did in the thirty-eight years that he resided at Pennhurst. After a carefully structured living experience, he is able to travel to work by bus, making two changes. He invites his mother regularly to breakfast on Sunday, and, in his mother's words, 'He looks like a million dollars.'

"Mrs. Auerbach testified that for one and a half years after the staff at Pennhurst had suggested moving him to a community-living arrangement she felt it was impossible and refused to allow the move. She did not believe he could be self-sufficient after all the years at Pennhurst, certainly not as severely retarded as he was. Yet she finally made the decision to allow the move, and all of her testimony to the court emphasized that she was pleased with the decision."

The judge to whom Grace Auerbach and other parents of children with mental retardation gave testimony concluded that often people are in institutions not because others wanted to put them there but because those who cared for them at the time had no other choices available. The decision to institutionalize a child with mental retardation is often difficult, and the parents do not want to be told they made the wrong decision or that the right decision is to place the child in the community and not institutionalization. Before they agree to a change, they want to be assured that community services will be ongoing and of good quality.

Since the 1960s, there has been a movement to de-institutionalize the care of mentally retarded adults, and place these patients in community living arrangements where they can function with minimal supervision.

Commented Gilhool: "Parents who committed their children to institutions approximately twenty-one years ago, when their children averaged thirteen years old, did so when no community alternatives existed. Coping with that decision and the chronic brutality that followed has enormous consequences for every parent. Some have withdrawn; some have embraced the institution and will adamantly defend it and their original decision. Others, those in the Associations for Retarded Citizens and other volunteer organizations, have worked long and hard to create alternatives so that other parents will not have to face such decisions."[1]

SUPPORTED LIVING
IN THE COMMUNITY

Current approaches to education of children with mental retardation include planning for independence as soon as the child's education begins.[2] Both social and sexual education are being emphasized, beginning in elementary school. This is in line with the trend toward supported living in the community for individuals with even the most challenging levels of mental retardation and related disabilities. Most advocacy groups now believe that people with mental retardation should live in homes and not in institutions. Commented one advocate for children and adults with mental retardation: "States have moved people [with mental retardation] into the community in large numbers. The discussions at the national level are on how to redirect federal money from institutions into the community and how to create new funding streams to support families who choose to keep their sons and daughters at home rather than in residential schools, large group homes, or other institutional settings. Likewise, we seek resources to support the adults who wish to live on their own but need supports in order to do so."

46

SOCIALLY APPROPRIATE BEHAVIOR

When a person with mental retardation is in his adolescent years, the question arises as to when he or she will be ready for the limited independence of some type of community living.[3] One of the skills that must be learned in order to make that possible is socially appropriate behavior. When *inappropriate* behavior is allowed to persist, even behavior that might seem harmless in some respects, it will tend to devalue a person with mental retardation and encourage others to think of him or her as a perpetual child.

Alastair Heron and Mary Myers, in their book, *Intellectual Impairment*, recounted an incident in which a minister had tolerantly endured "a painfully boisterous bear hug" every week after morning service from a woman with Down syndrome. In desperation, he decided to try a technique of his own. Before she could get her arms around him, he offered his hand in a warm, conventional handshake, which the woman, to his great relief, readily accepted. From then on, instead of a crushing bear hug, the minister was greeted with a handshake. This change in behavior did not go unnoticed by the congregation. In the weeks that followed, more and more members of the congregation came forward to shake hands with the woman. Commented the authors, "Her hugs, harmless if embarrassing to others, were definitely harmful to the social development of the lady herself. This intellectually disabled person was *socially handicapped* by being tacitly encouraged to continue childish activities into adult life."[4]

In addition to learning socially appropriate behavior, mentally retarded individuals need to learn all the self-help and survival skills that will make community living possible. They must be competent in caring for their needs in such areas as toileting, dressing, bathing, neatness of appearance, and general personal grooming. Full-time edu-

47

cation should not stop when a person with mental retardation has reached adolescence but continue into adulthood, as needed.

This need to continue with education and training may be quite obvious in a young person with Down syndrome who has only a moderate degree of mental retardation and who is beginning to read and write and handle money. But the need is even greater in an adolescent with a greater degree of mental retardation who has a short attention span and has not yet learned to sit for long and enjoy any sustained activity, who is bored and endlessly seeking human attention. The adolescent with mental retardation should always be given choice in such matters as clothing, bedtime, diet, and personal relationships. But whatever level of development has been reached, there is a constant need for stimulation and new experiences so that personal development can continue.

LEARNING
ABOUT DEATH

The death of a mentally retarded adolescent's parent can result in serious problems for the child who has not been taught how to accept death as a fact of life. Grief, anxiety, vulnerability, loneliness, and emotional pain are part of life. A child who has been sheltered from these experiences may have difficulty in expressing feelings of fear, anger, and bewilderment. When a parent dies, the grief that results is not just over the parent's death. It may also be associated with the loss of home, life-style, and all the ordinary familiar contacts if the child is taken from the home and placed in a community residence under the supervision of strangers. Furthermore, if the death is left unexplained by relatives in the belief that the child will soon forget all about it, the resulting fear and distress can mount to an unmanageable level.

In one reported instance, the widowed mother of a

pleasant fifteen-year-old boy with Down syndrome died suddenly. He had always lived with her, but when she died he was taken to a children's home, where his behavior changed markedly. By the time a week had passed, he had started swearing, exposing himself, and being aggressive. Authorities at the home moved quickly to admit this "aggressive mongol" to a hospital. Staff members there eventually learned that nobody had explained to the boy where his mother was or why he had been sent to the children's home. Nor had anyone taken the trouble to find out if the boy had any understanding of death. Until then no one had recognized his state of mourning or his need for counseling sessions.

REACTIONS TO
PAIN

Without help from parents and counseling when needed, a child with mental retardation can be easily frightened by pain, strangers, physical restraint, and raised voices.[5] This can sometimes interfere with attempts to give the child needed medical treatment. The following incident is a good example. A young boy with Down syndrome had an untreated medical problem for more than two years. The medical problem involved the inflammation and swelling of the foreskin of his penis. The boy was in pain, terrified, and had fought off all attempts to apply an ointment that had been prescribed by his physician. Finally, in desperation, his father brought him to a psychiatrist for help.

To calm him and give him some relief, the boy was given a long soak in the bathtub with some toys to play with. While he was thus distracted, the doctor chatted with him in a quiet manner. After a while he agreed to let the doctor apply some anesthetic jelly to the affected area. This removed the pain and the panic. It also cleared the way for the ultimate solution to the problem, a circumcision, which was performed a few days later.

EFFECTS OF
BRAIN DAMAGE

Various forms and degrees of brain damage associated with mental retardation can have an unpredictable effect on the moods, emotions, and thought processes of children and adults with mental retardation. This can sometimes result in anxiety states, severe depression, and obsessional behavior. This compounds the difficulties not only in providing them with needed medical treatment but also in teaching them self-help and survival skills. A great deal of behavior research has been done and continues in several basic areas, such as toileting and self-feeding. Both skills are necessary if any type of independent living is to be attained. Self-feeding skills, for example, encompass a variety of mealtime behaviors, including spoon-feeding, use of multiple utensils, cafeteria line skills, table manners, dining in restaurants, and cooking.[6]

Dressing and undressing are other basic skills that need to be mastered before independent living in the community is possible. These skills help to give those who are retarded more control over their lives, especially when learned in conjunction with regard for their personal appearance. The degree of skill learned will affect their social interactions with people who are not retarded. So will their skills in personal hygiene or grooming. These include bathing, brushing teeth, shaving, and hair care. One of the trends in teaching these skills is to train retarded individuals to evaluate their own progress and to give each other feedback. By interacting with their peers, they can share each other's struggles to learn and their successes.

VOCATIONAL TRAINING
AND PLACEMENT

Living independently in the community usually means a person with mental retardation must be able to work to provide money for living expenses.[7] This option used to be

50

considered available only to those who were mildly or moderately retarded, but advances in training techniques have extended this option to some who are severely retarded. They are being taught to perform complex, multistep tasks that involve objects of varying size, color, and shape with considerable success, providing they have sufficient manual dexterity. In fact, this type of training is an important measure of a mentally retarded person's chances for supported employment. So are certain kinds of intelligence and manual dexterity tests.

The results of the Stanford-Binet Intelligence Test have been found to correlate significantly with two tests of manual dexterity, the O'Connor Tweezer Dexterity Test and the Minnesota Rate of Manipulation Placing Test. Those who do well on the intelligence test usually do well on the manual dexterity tests. Also, when those tested score equally well on manual dexterity tests, those with the higher IQs are more likely to be successful. This is true whether they are working in a competitive job or in a supported employment situation.

When employment demand is high, individuals with mental retardation will be more likely to find employment in competitive work situations. This became apparent during World War II, when even those who had been institutionalized were released into the community to fill jobs left vacant by draftees. One case study showed 177 ex-residents of a mentally retarded care facility, the Wayne County Training School, living in the community in 1944 who would otherwise have not been considered ready to do this. This same study showed that more than 80 percent of these former residents were successfully participating in community life, the armed forces, in war industries, civilian jobs, or homemaking.

Studies of the employment success of those with mental retardation during World War II suggest that as economic opportunities increase, so do society's expectations with regard to the work competence of persons with mental

Many adults with mental retardation are eligible for assembly-line work in factories. A number are now being trained to perform jobs requiring more complicated tasks. Employment gives these individuals a greater sense of self-respect, and enables them to contribute more to the socio-economic life of their community.

retardation. In other words, when there is a need they tend to live up to society's expectations in meeting those needs. Past history also shows the reverse to be true. When the economy took a downturn, the opportunities for individuals with mental retardation to find work also dropped accordingly.

IMPORTANCE OF
WORK EXPERIENCE

Before enlightened changes improved the prospects of those with mental retardation, those who could not be cared for at home or who were heavily dependent on others were at risk of spending every day of their adult lives within the same four walls, with stultifying and depressing consequences. Fortunately, changes in attitude and practices have lessened the likelihood that many persons with mental retardation will have to spend their days within the rigid formats of institutions. They are now encouraged to become responsible, independent adults, and this includes preparation and training to perform work for pay. They are then not only contributing to the socio-economic life of the community in which they live, but are also given an opportunity to increase their self-respect.

The opportunity to be gainfully employed in a useful occupation can give mentally retarded people a great sense of achievement and self-worth that is unobtainable in any other activity. Those with mental retardation can be successful in many kinds of jobs. However, the training in appropriate skills must be adequate; they must respond well to work discipline; and they must demonstrate a capacity for sustained effort.

The cooperation of employers and the continued support of mental retardation professionals are also required. Among the jobs for which those with mental retardation are most eligible are assembly-line work in factories and service jobs in hotels, hospitals, and nursing homes. Wher-

The first U.S. Senate page
with mental retardation
sits on the steps
of the Capitol.

ever employment opportunities exist, however, the trend is to place as many persons with mental retardation as possible in jobs in the community. In this way they can help pay for their living expenses and attain a measure of pride in being able to support themselves. However, problems may soon develop if the work is not appropriate to the level of skill or the interests of the person with mental retardation.

For example, one man, whose learning difficulties were complicated by epilepsy and who had a tendency toward a hot temper, wanted a job in the heavy industry field that employed his father and brothers. This was a passionate but unrealistic desire because of his physical limitations, but it was the kind of "men's work" he wanted to do. When he was given training in domestic work he rebelled, goaded by his brothers, who teasingly referred to it as "woman's work." He expressed his contempt for it in aggressive outbursts. His sensitive pride made solutions to his work needs difficult to provide until his stress and anxiety were overcome. One solution would have been for him to find janitorial work in some male-dominated industry through a supported employment program.[8]

DEALING WITH
OBSESSIVE BEHAVIOR

Another case involved a young man with Down syndrome who had been receiving training in domestic work and liked it. His problems began when he was rotated out of the domestic training unit at the work center and given training in another kind of work. All of a sudden his behavior became bizarre. It included swearing, aggression, stripping, and self-induced vomiting. He had chewed his fingernails so much that they became infected. He was not eating and was therefore losing weight. His family reported that he was suffering from loss of sleep, loss of interest, and frequent weeping.

The crux of the problem was discovered to be that he had an obsessive/compulsive personality disorder. He liked his life in rigid routines and loved domestic work. When he was taken out of the domestic training rotation he became severely depressed because the routine he liked so much had been interrupted. When he was given antidepressant drugs he responded well, however, and this was followed up with programs to broaden his range of experience and reduce his obsessional activities, at home as well as at the work center.

SHARED PERSONAL RESOURCES

Behavior problems are a constant challenge to mental retardation professionals as well as to their clients, many of whom want very much to be able to perform useful work for pay. As they make progress they receive reinforcement from those who are training them. They also receive reinforcement from their peers. The emotional and practical support that friends are able to give each other can be a tremendous resource. They take a great deal of pleasure in regular work routines and can be taught ways to feel pride, no matter how humble their successes may appear to those who are not mentally retarded. This sharing of pride and emotional support encourages success and contributes to each individual's potential for attaining stability both on the job and in the community.

5

Health Problems and Treatment

Many people with mental retardation are afflicted by a wide range of health problems. Some are physiological and some psychological in origin. The majority of individuals with mental retardation do not have major behavioral problems. When serious problems do occur, however, treatment can be complicated by such behavior problems as easy irritability, anxiety, explosive tantrums, and other maladaptive behavior. When these difficulties occur, the affected individuals may be given drugs to calm them and to help control their behavior. However, given over a long period of time, these drugs may interfere with the body's use of the nutrients needed for good health.

The most commonly prescribed drugs are the anticonvulsants, psychotropic drugs, laxatives, antibiotics, and oral contraceptives. Over-the-counter, or nonprescription, drugs such as aspirin, antacids, and cold medicines are also used in treating minor health complaints.

Health problems can become even more difficult if the treatment is resisted or refused. In the case of adults, under the law the right to refuse treatment must be respected. However, it is sometimes difficult for doctors and other

57

health professionals to tell the difference between resistance and refusal. This is true even when a person's legal guardian has given informed consent. There is also a moral dilemma if such treatment as anesthesia, psychoactive drugs, or physical restraints are used. The guidelines set forth in each state for medical treatment of persons with mental retardation must be carefully followed and duly reported, with full respect of and adherence to their rights as defined by law.

EATING DISORDERS

The eating habits of the majority of those with mental retardation reflect the general population. However, harmful eating habits can be a significant health problem.[1] One study showed that 26 percent of a predominantly adult population in institutions for the mentally retarded had a problem called *pica*. This is the eating of nonfood items, such as clay and dirt, or the excessive eating of food. The greater the degree of retardation, the more common this practice was. This problem can also be aggravated by stress as well as by inadequate training in life skills. Another medical term for the eating of clay and dirt is *geophagia*. This can cause a lowering of serum iron and zinc levels in the body.

Even a marginal deficiency of zinc as a nutrient can lead to a decrease in the body's ability to heal wounds, as well as a decrease in general body growth. A deficiency of iron is considered to be one of the causes of increased irritability. Another danger of pica or geophagia is that nonfood items containing lead may be ingested, which can cause a host of complications. This practice may also expose people to parasitic infections of the gastrointestinal tract, which can interfere with the absorption of nutrients.

INFECTIOUS DISEASES

The spread of infectious diseases is a concern in any situation in which groups of people live together. The concern grows according to how serious the disease is. A common infectious disease found in institutions for individuals with mental retardation is hepatitis B virus. This disease attacks the liver and may cause jaundice, a yellowing of the skin and whites of the eyes. One study showed an incidence of from 60 to 80 percent of carriers of this virus in institutions for the mentally retarded. Carriers may not exhibit symptoms of the disease themselves, but they have the ability to infect others through personal contact. Persons with mental retardation who have not been taught how to control their behavior and other life skills may commit such physical acts as biting, indiscriminate kissing, and mouth-to-mouth sharing of food, all of which are means of spreading the disease. Other major factors in the spread of hepatitis B infection are poor sanitary conditions and the failure to provide sex education. Those most at risk are those with Down syndrome, about 40 percent of whom become carriers of the virus for indefinite periods of time (compared with 14 percent of the remaining mentally retarded population).

Another infectious disease in which the risk of transmission is greater in some institutions than it is in the general population is tuberculosis (TB), a disease caused by bacteria. The bacteria usually attack the lungs but can also spread to other parts of the body, in particular the brain, kidneys, and bones. This disease, once prevalent and usually fatal, is now successfully treated with antibiotics. In recent years it has become rare among the general population, although there are occasional isolated outbreaks. Two methods of detecting this disease are tuberculin skin tests and chest X rays for those whose skin test shows a positive reaction.

MEDICATION TO
CONTROL BEHAVIOR

Many persons with mental retardation have serious health problems that begin at birth or develop later, and these include a wide range of disabling illnesses. One characteristic that all persons with mental retardation share, however, due in part to frustration when they are not able to understand the world around them, is the problem of learning socially acceptable behavior. Behavior is usually more bizarre and disruptive among those in institutions than among those who live in community residential facilities, in foster group homes, or at home with parents. Behavior problems cited in institutions include hyperactivity, aggression, running, and self-destruction. In a study in one institution, about one-third of the residents exhibited some form of antisocial behavior, such as fighting, stealing, lying, and screaming, at least once a month. Through lack of attention and stimulation, they often lose interest in their environment. Occasionally the behavior is aggressive and destructive enough to require some form of therapy.[2]

Behavior problems exhibited in community residential facilities are usually not as severe or widespread, but they do exist. Among the problems cited of those with mild or moderate retardation are low frustration tolerance, hyperactivity, aggression, and problems having to do with motivation. Individuals have a tendency to become depressed when they feel inadequate and hopeless, or when they are rejected by their peers and others. Whatever the degree of mental retardation, any tendency toward behavior problems is aggravated when there is a lack of training and support in learning life skills, including age-appropriate behavior.[3]

When a person with mental retardation exhibits behavior problems, the most frequently prescribed medication is one of the *antipsychotic drugs*, such as a tranquilizer or neuroleptic. Some studies have shown that about half of all residents in institutions for the mentally retarded may be on antipsychotic drugs at any one time. The same holds true for residents of community foster and group homes. However, the use of these drugs for students with mental retardation who attend special education classes is much less frequent. These drugs are most often prescribed for aggressive, destructive, hyperactive, and antisocial behavior. None of the drugs used is completely successful in controlling behavior, although there is often some improvement.[4]

Improvement in behavior aside, however, the use of these drugs may have a negative effect on the person's ability to learn by interfering with attention and memory. Studies have also shown that there is a tendency to give stronger doses than necessary. In a study of one commonly prescribed antipsychotic drug it was found that giving half the standard dosage was just as effective in controlling behavior. Concern has also been raised about the potential for harmful side effects.

When there is a need to control serious behavior problems, antipsychotic drugs can be useful when given in moderation and when the dosage is carefully monitored to avoid harmful side effects. When given to children, immediate side effects are rare, but in the long term they can be quite serious, affecting not only body growth but the ability to learn. When certain types of this medication are withdrawn, this can sometimes result in physical problems such as spotting of the retina, the innermost layer of the eye that helps control vision. Withdrawal can also sometimes trigger seizures.

Another possible side effect is called tardive dyskinesia. This is a movement disorder characterized by involuntary, rhythmic, and repetitive movements of the face, mouth, and extremities. The incidence is thought to be relatively high. In one study of 103 children who had been on long-term therapy with phenothiazine, a neuroleptic drug, 20 percent were found to have tardive dyskinesia. This side effect is particularly serious because there is no effective treatment. It tends to be a permanent condition and interferes with adaptive behavior. The aim of current research in the use of antipsychotic drugs and their side effects, in particular tardive dyskinesia, is to identify those persons who are most at risk. Other aims are to determine the safest dosage ranges and drug types and to develop appropriate forms of treatment.

PSYCHOTHERAPY

From the very beginnings of treatment for children and adults with mental retardation, some form of psychotherapy was used. This was true of the French pioneers Itard and Seguin, even though the principles of psychotherapy had not been established at that time. However, when psychology came to be recognized as a science in the late nineteenth century, attention began to be focused on how this new science could be used to help those with mental retardation. In the early decades of the twentieth century, many child guidance clinics were established. These clinics dealt with large numbers of children with mental retardation. At about this time psychotherapeutic methods began to be used in treating children and adults in state institutions. However, as the number of patients in state institutions increased, this effort became less and less successful. Instead, attention began to be focused on training and rehabilitation.

The 1960s saw the beginning of the movement against institutionalization of those with mental retardation. With the emphasis on some form of community living arrangement, the need and the opportunities for psychotherapeutic treatment grew. So did a consensus as to the best approach to use in treating children and adults with mental retardation. It was agreed that the therapist should have a positive attitude and believe at least in the possibility that a patient with mental retardation could improve through treatment. A planned approach should be used that includes goals, although they must of necessity be limited.

One of the most important goals in therapy for children and adults with mental retardation is to help them improve their behavior so they can enjoy greater social acceptability. Depending on the patient, this may be as simple as removing an annoying behavior trait. Or it may involve efforts to help the patient become more emotionally mature and have a greater sense of self-worth. These and other goals are vital if the person under treatment is to reach the ultimate goal of being able to live a life of limited independence.

Emotional ties are an essential part of the patient's psychological environment. These ties exist whether the patient lives with family, in a group home, or in some other kind of residential setting. Any ties to family are emotional ties. For this reason it may be necessary and beneficial to involve members of the immediate family and any other relatives who have a close relationship with the patient.

ART, MUSIC, AND OTHER THERAPIES

When psychotherapy by itself does not bring the desired results, sometimes other therapies are used in conjunction with it. These may include art, music, dance, and movement therapies, all of which can be helpful, especially for those who cannot communicate well with words. The goal is not to make the person with mental retardation proficient in art or music or dance, but to improve the person's behavior and ability to learn. All of these therapies tend to improve social skills as well as motor development—the ability to use hands skillfully and move about gracefully. They encourage more self-confidence and improve ability to communicate with others. They also contribute to the patient's understanding of how he or she fits into the environment both physically and emotionally.

LEARNING SELF-HELP SKILLS

One of the first and most important skills for a person with mental retardation to learn is toileting. The unpleasantness of toileting accidents, the amount of time and effort needed to clean mental retardation clients, and the humiliation involved have prompted extensive research on how best to solve this problem. In addition to learning how to control

*Sometimes alternate treatments,
such as art, music, or physical
therapy, are necessary to help
improve the behavior of
individuals who cannot communicate
well with words and therefore
do not respond to psychotherapy.*

the bodily functions of urination and bowel movements and to maintain personal cleanliness, the mentally retarded are taught many other self-help skills. Among them are dressing and undressing, toothbrushing, bathing, hand washing, grooming, shoe tying, bed making, and feeding. Like other good social and behavioral skills, these are basic requirements if a person with mental retardation is to be able to achieve the goal of living independently in the community.

6
Prevention and Research

A man and a woman get married because they love each other and want to spend their lives together. If they are both in good health, they may also want children so they can experience what it means to be a family, sharing their love, their goals, and aspirations with each other and with their children. When a child is born with mental retardation and there is no history of mental retardation in either parent's family, they may experience shock and anguish. They may even go through a grieving process. However, not all parents are traumatized by giving birth to a child with mental retardation. One mental retardation professional recounted an instance in which a parent characterized the experience "as planning to take a trip to Germany but ending up in France. It may be a different country, but it is still Europe. You just have to learn another language and way of life."

However, parents who have produced a child with mental retardation and hope to produce a normal child together will probably seek help from a *genetic counselor.*[1] This is a specialist in inherited diseases. The counselor will take a detailed medical history of both parents and their families. Tests will be made of blood and other bodily fluids to find out what dominant and recessive traits each parent has inherited. When all of this work has been completed, the couple will have the information they need to help them decide whether or not to have another child.

These are the essential aspects of genetic counseling: (1) providing facts about the inheritance of genetic diseases; (2) suggesting tests that will provide information about each parent's genetic makeup; and (3) informing the couple about the likelihood that they will produce a child with mental retardation.

If they have already produced a child with this disability, the counselor is trained to help them and their families to cope and adjust. When the problem is first discussed, it can become a heavy emotional burden. The parents may suddenly feel overpowering guilt, denial, anger, and other deep anxieties. They may blame themselves or each other, even though neither is to blame for their misfortune. When they conceived the child they may not have had any knowledge whatsoever of the possibility that the child might be born with mental retardation.

The couple may be in such shock at the first session that they may not hear what is being said. At least one more session may be needed so the couple will be able to give full attention to the counselor's discussion of why the child was born retarded and what the chances may be of their producing another child with mental retardation. It is also important for the couple to ask questions so they can eliminate any unnecessary fears and make it a positive, give-and-take session.

After the second session the couple should be well enough informed to decide whether or not to have another child. Another essential part of the counseling process is to introduce parents to sources of help that may be needed throughout the life of their child. This will include information about early-intervention programs, therapy, support groups, parent organizations, and appropriate social service agencies.

OPTIONS AVAILABLE
TO PARENTS

Any couple who has produced a child with mental retardation will have certain options to consider regarding any future children. These will depend on the type of genetic disorder involved and the risk of recurrence. They must also be aware of the emotional, financial, and physical burdens they may have to assume if they produce another disabled child. There are no clear-cut guidelines. One couple may view a 1 percent risk as too great, while another may consider a 25 percent risk as one with relatively good odds.

A couple that doesn't want to take the chance of producing a child with mental retardation may practice birth control. Or if they want another child, they can adopt one. Sterilization of the man or the woman, thus preventing conception, is another option. If the couple approves of abortion, they may use that option if the woman becomes pregnant and the prenatal diagnosis indicates that the child will be born abnormal. Or they may simply take the risk and play the odds, hoping that their next child will be born normal.

DIAGNOSIS BY
AMNIOCENTESIS

When a woman becomes pregnant and there are risks of certain types of genetic defects, such as biochemical abnormalities, chromosomal anomalies, or neural tube defects, she may ask her physician for a prenatal diagnosis by means of *amniocentesis*.[2] This procedure is usually performed about the sixteenth week of pregnancy and involves the use of a syringe to withdraw a small amount of the amniotic fluid surrounding the fetus. This fluid contains fetal cells that can be tested to find out if they contain any of the above-mentioned defects.

This test can be reassuring to couples who have had children with a chromosome abnormality or a neural tube defect because the chance of a recurrence is usually no more than 1 to 3 percent. It may be a different story for those at risk of producing a child with a biochemical disease. A risk of 25 percent may be too great to plan another pregnancy unless they use amniocentesis to decide whether or not to terminate the pregnancy.

Couples who run the risk of producing a child with X-linked mental retardation, which only affects males, may decide to use amniocentesis so they can produce only normal female children. In other words, a couple who elects to use amniocentesis must be prepared for the possibility of having to make a decision whether or not to terminate a pregnancy if they approve of abortion. This is a difficult decision in any case, but particularly so in the case of X-linked disorders. Only half of male fetuses will be affected by this disorder; the other half will be born normal.

Amniocentesis itself is not without risks. This procedure carries with it the threat of miscarriage or injury to the fetus. Sometimes couples who have a child with mental retardation for which no cause can be found will request an amniocentesis when the woman again becomes pregnant. They want to be sure that the baby will be born normal. However, when no cause is known, the risk of producing another child with mental retardation is estimated at 6 percent. Even if the diagnosis by amniocentesis is normal, however, the chance that the child will be born with mental retardation cannot be ruled out. The procedure is not foolproof. It can only rule out chromosome disorders and neural tube defects. In other words, the possible .5 percent risk of miscarriage from an amniocentesis is much greater than the .1 percent chance that the child might be born with Down syndrome, a condition for which they do not have

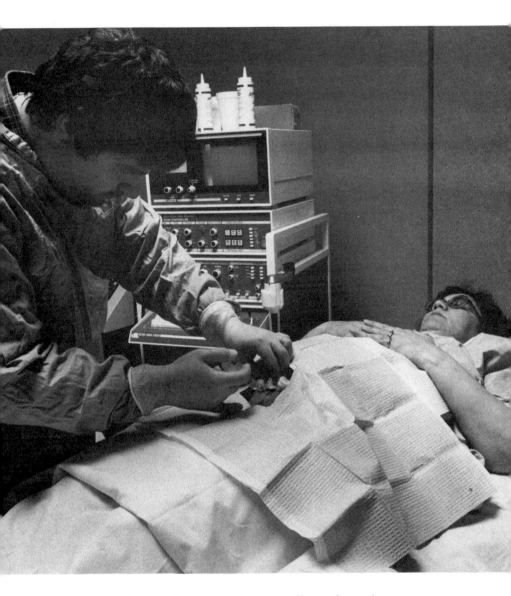

*Amniocentesis, a procedure usually performed on
women during the sixteenth week of pregnancy,
can help diagnose certain genetic disorders
present in the fetus such as Down syndrome.*

an increased risk. In those circumstances, amniocentesis would not in any way be beneficial.

RESEARCH FOR
A BETTER LIFE

One of the pervading questions in research about mental retardation is: How can we make a better life for children and adults with mental retardation?[3] This question is more complicated than it might seem, because there are two ways to look at it. One is from a moral point of view: what is meant by "a better life"? The other is more practical or technological: What is the most efficient way to make life more pleasant and rewarding for those who are disabled mentally and, often, physically as well? Both of these questions must be considered in any discussion of how life can be made better for those with mental retardation.

At the beginning of the twentieth century most people believed the way to provide a better life was to put the mentally retarded in institutions that would give them the special services they needed. The environment should be emotionally supportive, and they should have access to all of the technology that could be provided for their self-improvement. The intention was for them to live comfortably among their peers in "an environment whose complexity was suitable to the individual's ability level."

The failures and abuses of this approach led eventually to the present attitude that retarded people should be provided with as close to normal an environment as possible. One of the essential elements of this argument is that they should remain in the community among family and friends. A "better life" for them must include a sense of being part of the larger society. When it isn't possible for a person who is mentally retarded to take his or her place in society alone, then society must provide the support needed to make this possible. It should be emphasized, however, that when those with mental retardation are en-

72

*A man with Down syndrome enjoys rock climbing.
Perhaps none of us know yet how high people
with mental retardation can aspire.*

couraged to take their place in society, they must be able to master certain basic social skills to make this possible.

WHY ARE SOME PEOPLE
SMARTER THAN OTHERS?

A second basic question in mental retardation research is: Why are some people smarter than others? The goal is to be able to come up with a satisfactory explanation for the observed differences between those who are mentally retarded and children and adults who do not have this disability. Another concern is how to measure the importance of biological versus environmental factors on intelligence. In many cases the cause of mental retardation can be traced to biological factors, including those discussed in earlier chapters, such as chromosome abnormalities, neural tube defects, and brain damage. But environment can also make a difference in a person's intelligence level.

This environment includes parents, brothers, sisters, and friends who have the potential to encourage and guide a person to act intelligently. For example, parents who encourage their children to ask questions and seek answers, who encourage their children to do their homework and perform well at school can make a difference by setting high standards. Learning involves effort and concentration, and the results are indicators of intelligence. In a similar way, professionals who train and educate persons with mental retardation in basic skills can make a difference in the results achieved when they provide a positive environmental influence.

As pointed out earlier, the first major breakthrough in intelligence testing was made by the Frenchman, Alfred Binet (1857–1911). As an experimental psychologist, Binet performed extensive research on perception, memory, and language. Much of this research was conducted on his own children as well as on children in public schools. In 1895 Binet founded a journal devoted to this type of research. He also founded a society in which other psychologists could contribute and discuss their ideas. From 1905 to 1908 he published the results of his studies on human intelligence.

Binet and other members of the society he founded were shocked at the treatment of children and adults with mental retardation in France at that time. In a major effort to remedy the situation they drafted a resolution to the French Ministry of Public Instruction in which they proposed the development of an intelligence test. The purpose of the test would be to distinguish those children requiring special educational help from those who were able to benefit from the educational system as it then existed. In this resolution they also proposed a special education demonstration project that would provide help to those children who needed it.

When the resolution was accepted, Binet's society was given responsibility for carrying out its provisions. The test that Binet and his colleagues developed was successful in showing the differences between children with mental retardation and those of normal intelligence. It also provided a means of predicting the degree to which a person might succeed in school. However, it could not show how the mentally retarded could be helped in developing their learning abilities.

Nonetheless it was considered a great step forward in attempts to understand intelligence and provide indicators of mental retardation. It also stimulated a great number of research questions in Europe and the United States. Chief among them was: What characteristics are associated with differences in test scores? Comparisons were made between individuals who scored high on a test and those who scored low. Family traits, environmental influences, and the physical disabilities of the subjects, if any, were compared and evaluated.

Later research would show that the child with mental retardation could learn and remember material in an experimental situation but with much more difficulty than subjects with normal intelligence. Also, a child with mental retardation had much more difficulty in recalling learned material because of defects in the ability to memorize or remember.

This led to the Box Model theory. This theory described the flow of information through the mind as a series of boxes, with each box representing a separate stage or process. One demonstration of this theory showed that information flowed in three steps, from (1) very short-term memory to storage in primary memory, (2) then to secondary memory, and (3) finally to tertiary memory. Each stage represented a greater degree of permanence or a capacity to remember something learned or experienced longer.

When this model was tested it suggested that the mechanism for moving information from primary memory to secondary memory, and for maintaining it in primary memory, was deficient in those with mental retardation. There was little difference in the first step, primary memory storage, between those with mental retardation and those with normal intelligence. But there was a great deal of difference where the second step, secondary memory, was concerned.

Many other tests based on the Box Model theory and others like it concluded that everything in the information-processing system of a person with mental retardation was deficient. This led to disenchantment with this type of theory because it produced no greater understanding of why some people are smarter than others than had the catalog approach in which simple differences were listed.

Continuing research on intelligence is becoming more sophisticated and holds promise for the future discovery of better ways to help those with mental retardation learn basic skills.

7
Protecting the Rights of People with Mental Retardation

The closing decades of the twentieth century have witnessed revolutionary changes in attitudes and laws governing the rights of children and adults with mental retardation. Through state and federal legislation and U.S. Supreme Court decisions, individuals with mental retardation are guaranteed rights that are commensurate in many ways with the rights guaranteed to all other citizens. A good example of this is the Pineland Decree of 1978 in Maine, which is considered one of the most progressive states in providing rights and privileges for those with mental retardation. This decree, implemented by the state legislature, declared:

"It is the intent of the Legislature to guarantee individual dignity, liberty, pursuit of happiness and the protection of the civil and legal rights of mentally retarded persons and to articulate rights of mentally retarded persons, so that these rights may be exercised and protected. Each mentally retarded person is entitled to the rights enjoyed by citizens of the state and of the United States, unless some of these rights have been suspended as the result of court guardianship proceedings" (when a person with mental retardation has been judged legally incompetent to make his or her own decisions).[1]

In Maine and other progressive states, the independence and productivity of persons with mental retardation are encouraged by providing *habilitation*, education, and other training in order to maximize their potential to lead independent and productive lives. Among the basic rights addressed are the rights to humane care; the practice of religion of their choice; communication, including the right to receive, send, and mail sealed, unopened correspondence; the right to work; and the right to vote (unless under guardianship).

The right to medical care is also clearly spelled out. For example, in Maine the law states that "each client is entitled to receive prompt and appropriate medical and dental treatment and care for physical and mental ailments and for the prevention of any illness or disability, and medical treatment shall be consistent with the accepted standards of medical practice in the community, unless the religion of the client so prohibits." *Client* refers to any person with mental retardation receiving services from the state bureau of mental retardation or from an agency or facility licensed or funded to provide services to mentally retarded persons, "except those presently serving sentences for crime." This latter point underscores the fact that when a person with mental retardation who is adjudged legally competent commits a crime he or she must suffer the consequences, just as other citizens must.

CONTROLLING THE
LIVES OF CHILDREN

Persons with mental retardation may be experiencing new rights and freedoms in many states, but they are still subject to the control and influence of others. This is particularly true in the case of children with mental retardation. Those most in control of the lives of children with mental retardation are physicians and educators, both of whom are

78

primarily responsible for designating a child as "mentally retarded." The physician has the ability to prevent mental retardation by counseling parents who are at risk. He also has the power to intervene early so that its effects can be minimized.

When a child is born with mental retardation, the physician can be a sustaining force throughout that person's life. The physician's decision as to whether a child is mentally retarded is based on developmental testing of the newborn and infants. The child who is developmentally delayed is the one who becomes classified as mentally retarded. This is most likely to happen, of course, if the child is severely or profoundly retarded rather than moderately or mildly retarded.

Educators also classify children. In fact, according to some researchers, schools label more children as mentally retarded than any other public or private agency. To be so classified has tremendous consequences, both positive and negative, in particular for a child whose mental retardation may be open to question. Some children have already been labeled "mentally retarded" before they enter school, but others become known or classified as such only when the schools label them as "different," "special," "exceptional," or otherwise different from what is considered normal.

Critics of those responsible for classifying children and adults as mentally retarded have called into question the practice of accepting anything as true and unassailable as long as it is presented as being scientific. They point out that some of the policies in effect regarding persons with mental retardation are not always based on *good* science. Therefore the policies are not always good. As an example, one critic recalled that at one time science taught that people with mental retardation were a menace to society. As a result of this "scientific" stance there was a movement to force children and adults with mental retardation into institutions and to sterilize them so they could not conceive children. Also called into question is the fallibility of many "scientific" tests of intelligence or of the potential for success in school.

Nonscientific judgments can also be devastating to a child. For instance, educators may classify as "mentally handicapped" students who are hard to handle. Critics have also protested that more often it is boys who are subjected to special education classification rather than girls, aggressive students more than the acquiescent, and students of racial and ethnic minorities more than white students. All of these judgments have legal implications.

One of the major reasons that the Education for All Handicapped Children Act was passed in 1975 was to clarify the methods and legal issues involved when a child is classified as mentally retarded or in need of special education. Under this act it is not possible to rely solely on "scientific" assessment measures, such as IQ tests. "Soft" data, such as teacher observations and functional skills, must also be used before a student is evaluated and classified as mentally retarded.

The laws in some states support this approach to classification by declaring that a person—child or adult—cannot be declared mentally incompetent unless the judgment is verified. Assessments by medical, psychological, and social workers must clearly show that the person's incompetence is the result of mental retardation, among other causes. All of these efforts, whether at the national or state level, are attempts to prevent people from being unnecessarily stigmatized as mentally retarded, with all of its social and legal implications.

DECISIONS AFFECTING LEGAL RIGHTS

Some of the earlier U.S. Supreme Court decisions involving persons with mental retardation were severely criticized because they sanctioned depriving children with mental retardation of rights that normal children have, such as the right to liberty and the right to an unharmful life in an institution. For example, referring to the *Parham* case (1979), which involved the liberty of children, and the *Pennhurst* case (1981), in which a decision on the right-to-treatment issue was ignored, authors H. Rutherford Trumbull III and Mary J. Wheat commented that both cases had disastrous consequences for people with mental retardation. They sanctioned the deprivation of normal legal rights. They deprived mentally retarded children of liberty, autonomy, and dignity by allowing them to be confined on a basis that would not justify the confinement of people without mental retardation. Stated the authors, "The cases thereby perpetuated a dual system of law, one that treats mentally retarded people more harshly solely because they are mentally retarded."[2]

PROGRESS IN PROTECTING RIGHTS

Even though advocates of the rights of those with mental retardation were extremely critical of some earlier Supreme Court decisions, the fact is that considerable progress has been made in achieving and protecting the rights of those with mental retardation, especially since the 1970s, with a tremendous upsurge in the 1980s. One of the key legal decisions, for example, centered around the treatment rights of a resident of Pennhurst State School and Hospital in Pennsylvania. This is the same institution that figured in an earlier, unfavorable U.S. Supreme Court decision. However, this time the Court of Appeals upheld the treatment rights of Pennhurst resident Nicholas Romeo, a thirty-year-old man with profound mental retardation. He had been involuntarily committed to the institution in 1974.

Advocates on his behalf filed a lawsuit in which they charged that Romeo had been "improperly shackled" and denied adequate protection and appropriate treatment. When the case came to trial, the Court of Appeals directed that the jury be instructed that under the due process clause of the Fourteenth Amendment to the U.S. Constitution, "shackling may be justified only by a compelling necessity, i.e., that the shackling was essential to protect the patient or to treat him. . . . '' The jury was also instructed that except in emergency situations the arguments that it was done because of inadequate resources or because of administrative policy are insupportable. They do not justify "intrusions of this kind on a fundamental liberty interest."

Like the earlier Pennhurst case, the case involving Nicholas Romeo was appealed to the U.S. Supreme Court. This time, however, the highest court in the land handed down a distinctly positive ruling concerning the rights of persons with mental retardation. It ruled that persons with mental retardation in state institutions have a constitutional right under the Fourteenth Amendment to safe conditions, freedom from unreasonable restraint, and at least "minimally adequate" training in caring for themselves. One of the most important arguments considered in the Court's deliberations was that since even convicted criminals have these rights, individuals with mental retardation, "who may not be punished at all," are entitled to at least as much legal protection.

THE REAL AND THE IDEAL

No matter what their level of mental retardation, whether living independently or enjoying the limited freedom of living in a community residential facility, it is evident that the rights of individuals with mental retardation are dependent on current laws and legal interpretations. Tremendous progress has been made in promoting independence and self-respect, but it is difficult indeed for persons with mental retardation to overcome long-standing fear and prejudice from more fortunate members of the community.

Even with newly won rights and privileges, the real world is still a very difficult and fragile world for the person with mental retardation. The ideal world would be one in which the rights advocated by the International League of Societies for the Mentally Handicapped are fully recognized and implemented in all of the United States and throughout the world. In 1968 this organization published

82

The Declaration of General and Specific Rights of the Mentally Retarded. This document states:

1. The person with mental retardation has the same basic rights as other citizens of the same country and age.
2. The person with mental retardation has a right to proper medical care, education, and training, so that he or she can develop to the fullest, no matter how severe the mental and physical handicaps may be.
3. The persons with mental retardation has a right to work and to maintain a decent standard of living.
4. The person with mental retardation has the right to live with his or her own family or with foster parents. He or she also has the right to take part in community activities, including leisure-time activities.
5. If it is necessary for a person with mental retardation to be cared for in a public or private institution, the care should provide as close to normal living conditions as possible.
6. If advisable, the person with mental retardation should have the right to be cared for by a guardian who will protect his or her personal well-being and interest.
7. The person with mental retardation has the right to protection from abuse and from being taken advantage of.
8. If a person with mental retardation is accused of having broken a law, that person has a right to a fair trial, with special regard given to his or her degree of responsibility.
9. Like all other citizens, the person with mental retardation should have the right to appeal to higher authorities if they, their families, or their guardians believe they have been treated unjustly.[3]

Glossary

Amniocentesis. A medical test usually performed about the sixteenth week of pregnancy. A syringe is used to withdraw a small amount of amniotic fluid, which contains fetal cells that are examined for evidence of biochemical or chromosomal abnormalities or neural tube defects that can cause mental retardation and other disabilities.

Antipsychotic drugs. A group of drugs, including tranquilizers and neuroleptics, that may be prescribed to help control serious behavior problems.

Apgar score. A test given to newborns in which heart rate, cry, muscle tone, color, and reflexes are tested and scored. Many newborns who score poorly will be mentally retarded.

Binet-Simon Intelligence Scale. A test designed in 1905 by the French psychologist Alfred Binet and his student, Theodore Simon, to measure memory, reasoning ability, the ability to compare objects, numerical skills, knowledge of common objects and ideas, and other indicators of intelligence. This test was also used to identify schoolchildren with mental retardation.

Chromosomes. Sub-units within the nucleus of each human cell that contain genetic material. In the normal human being there are twenty-three pairs of chromosomes, with one chromosome in each pair coming from the mother and one from the father.

Client. Any person with mental retardation who receives services from a state bureau of mental retardation or from an agency or facility licensed or funded to provide services to persons with mental retardation, except those who are serving sentences for crime.

Congenital syphilis. A sexually transmitted disease. In a pregnant woman, it can cause inflammation of the membranes enclosing the brain and spinal cord and accumulation of fluid in the brain of her unborn child.

Cytomegalovirus. An infection in the mother's womb that destroys nervous tissue and interferes with the development of the fetus's brain.

Down syndrome. A form of mental retardation and accompanying physical defects caused by a chromosome disorder, the most common being trisomy 21, in which chromosome 21 has three chromosomes instead of the normal two.

Genetic counselor. A specialist in inherited diseases who counsels parents, through the use of medical tests and studies of family medical histories, about the likelihood that they might produce a child with mental retardation or another disability.

Geophagy. A medical term for the eating of clay and dirt.

Habilitation. The process by which persons with mental retardation are assisted to acquire and maintain life skills enabling them (1) to cope with the demands of their own person and environment, (2) to raise the level of their physical, mental, and social deficiency, and (3) to upgrade their sense of well-being, including but not limited to programs of formal, structured education and treatment.

Hepatitis B virus. A disease that attacks the liver and may cause jaundice, a yellowing of the skin and whites of the eyes.

Herpes simplex virus. A sexually transmitted disease. When present in a pregnant woman's vagina, it can cause inflammation of the membranes that enclose the newborn's brain and spinal cord, massive hemorrhage, and destruction of brain tissue.

Informed consent. Consent voluntarily given with sufficient knowledge and comprehension of the subject matter involved so as to enable the person giving consent to make an understanding and enlightened decision without any element of force, fraud, deceit, duress, or other form of constraint or coercion.

Lesch-Nyhan syndrome. An X-linked recessive disorder that causes mental retardation, a form of cerebral palsy, and a compulsion for self-mutilation.

Mental retardation. A condition in which a person is below average in his or her ability to learn. He or she will have difficulty in learning some, but not necessarily all, adaptive skills. Mental retardation begins prior to age eighteen but may not always be of lifelong duration.

Myotonic dystrophy. A disease caused by an abnormal dominant gene, marked by varying degrees of mental retardation as well as muscular dystrophy and difficulty in relaxing contracted muscles, especially those in the jaws and hands.

Neural tube defects. A cause of mental retardation involving the interaction of several defective genes. Among the birth defects associated with this condition are anencephaly, a severe and fatal defect in brain development; encephalocele, in which brain tissue protrudes through a defect in the cranium; and spina bifida, in which part of the bony spine that helps protect the spinal cord fails to develop.

Otis Group Test of Mental Ability. A test developed in 1916 by Arthur S. Otis, an American psychologist, the first of its kind that did not have to be administered to one subject at a time. Later developments included the Otis Group Intelligence Scale and the Otis Self-Administering Test of Mental Ability.

Pica. The harmful practice of eating nonfood items such as clay and dirt or the excessive eating of food.

Public Law 94-142. A federal law that guarantees that all citizens with disabilities, including mental retardation, will receive appropriate education from age three to age twenty one. The education must be individualized for the child. Also, all students with disabilities must be integrated or "mainstreamed" into regular education programs to the maximum extent possible.

Residential facility. A facility that provides twenty-four-hour residential care for persons with mental retardation and which is owned, operated, licensed, or funded in whole or in part by a state bureau of mental retardation or department of human services.

Rubella (German measles). A contagious viral disease. In a pregnant woman, it can cause defects in the fetus's eyes, ears, heart, and brain, resulting in mental retardation along with other serious disabilities.

Stanford-Binet Intelligence Test. A revision and refinement of the Binet-Simon Intelligence Scale. Initiated in 1916 by the American psychologist Lewis M. Terman, this test has undergone several revisions and is still in use today.

Von Recklinghausen's disease. A disease caused by an abnormal dominant gene, marked by skin lesions in the form of oval-shaped patches of light brown color, curvature of the spine, a larger than normal head, and nodules both on and under the skin. About 12 percent of persons with this disease have seizures and about 10 percent are mentally retarded.

Wechsler Intelligence Scale for Children (1949) and the Wechsler Adult Intelligence Scale (1955). Tests designed by American psychologist David Wechsler. His tests provide three distinct IQs: one for the entire test, one for the group consisting of verbal skills, and one for performance tests.

X-linked recessive disorders. A cause of mental retardation due to an abnormal recessive gene located on an X chromosome that comes from the mother and affecting only male children (who receive a Y chromosome from the father to complete the pair, which determines the sex of the child).

Source Notes

CHAPTER 1 MYTHS AND FACTS

1. American Association on Mental Retardation, memorandum from Committee on Terminology and Classification concerning proposed revisions, September 21, 1990, pp. 2–4.

2. Joey case history from personal interview with brother of person with mental retardation, Newcastle, Maine, April 1990.

3. Alastair Heron and Mary Myers, *Intellectual Impairment* (London and New York: Academic Press, 1983), pp. 7–15 and 22–36.

CHAPTER 2 CAUSES OF MENTAL RETARDATION

1. American Association on Mental Retardation, memorandum from Committee on Terminology and Classification concerning proposed revisions, Sept. 21, 1990, Section IV, pp. 6–9.

2. Robert E. Dunbar, *Heredity* (New York: Franklin Watts, Inc., 1978), pp. 27–36, 38–42.

3. Johnny L. Matson and James A. Mulick, eds., *Handbook of Mental Retardation* (Elmsford, N.Y.: Pergamon Press Inc., 1983), pp. 97–101, 105–119, 121–139.

4. Personal interview with and notes provided by Chester Halsey Hill, counselor and case manager, Mobius Activity Center for adults with mental retardation, Newcastle, Maine, November 1990.

CHAPTER 3 OPPORTUNITIES FOR EDUCATION AND
TRAINING
1. Personal interview with and notes provided by Chester Halsey
Hill, counselor and case manager, Mobius Activity Center for adults
with mental retardation, Newcastle, Maine, November 1990.
2. Matson and Mulick, pp. 67–75, 171–181.
3. *Encyclopedia Americana*, 1989, "Intelligence Testing," pp.
241–245.
4. Facts and commentary provided by Celane M. McWhorter,
Alexandria, Virginia, an advocate for children and adults with mental
retardation, October 1990.

CHAPTER 4 THE QUALITY OF LIFE
1. Philip Roos, Brian M. McCann, and Max R. Addison, eds.
*Shaping the Future, Community-Based Residential Services and Facil-
ities for Mentally Retarded People* (Baltimore: University Park Press,
1980), pp. 9–10.
2. Personal interview with and notes provided by Francesca Pa-
taro, Community Program Consultant, Maine Bureau of Mental Retardation, November 1990, and correspondence from Celane M. Mc-
Whorter, advocate for children and adults with mental retardation,
October 1990.
3. Heron and Myers, pp. 16–21, 32–40.
4. Ibid., pp. 30, 37–38.
5. Ibid., p. 44.
6. Matson and Mulick, pp. 434–439.
7. Ibid. pp. 192–196, 455–461.
8. Heron and Myers, pp. 41–47.

CHAPTER 5 HEALTH PROBLEMS AND TREATMENT
1. Matson and Mulick, pp. 282–284, 292–299.
2. Ibid, pp. 319–324.
3. Personal interviews with and notes provided by Francesca Pa-
taro, Community Program Consultant, and Chester Halsey Hill, counselor and case manager.
4. Matson and Mulick, pp. 325–332, 354–359.

CHAPTER 6 PREVENTION AND RESEARCH
1. Matson and Mulick, pp. 266–268.
2. *American Medical Association Family Medical Guide* (New
York: Random House, 1987), p. 653.
3. Matson and Mulick, pp. 143–154, 527–538.

CHAPTER 7 PROTECTING THE RIGHTS OF PEOPLE WITH
MENTAL RETARDATION
1. From Pineland Decree of 1978 in Maine and resulting laws,
regulations, and guidelines.
2. Matson and Mulick, pp. 79–90, 157–168.
3. International League of Societies for the Mentally Handicapped, *The Declaration of General and Specific Rights of the Mentally
Retarded*, 1968.

For Further Reading

American Association on Mental Retardation. *Terminology
and Classification Manual*, Revised Edition. Wash-
ington, D.C., 1991.
Dunbar, Robert E. *Heredity*. New York: Franklin Watts,
Inc., 1978.
Edgerton, Robert B. *Mental Retardation*. Cambridge,
Mass.: Harvard University Press, 1979.
Heron, Alastair, and Myers, Mary. *Intellectual Impair-
ment*. New York: Academic Press, 1983.
Matson, Johnny L., and Mulick, James A., eds. *Handbook
of Mental Retardation*. Elmsford, N.Y.: Pergamon
Press, 1983.
Roos, Philip; McCann, Brian M.; and Addison, Max K.
*Shaping the Future—Community-Based Residential
Services and Facilities for Mentally Retarded People*.
Baltimore: University Park Press, 1980.

Index

Movement therapy, 63
Music therapy, 63, *64-65*
Mutations, 18
Myers, Mary, 47
Myotonic dystrophy, 18–19

National Association for
    Retarded Children, 28
Neural tube defects, 20, 70
Newborns, tests for, 23

Obsessional behavior, 55–56
O'Connor Tweezer
    Dexterity Test, 51
Otis, Arthur S., 33–34
Overprotectiveness, 13, 16
Oxygen deprivation, 23

Pain, reactions to, 49
Parents:
    death of, 48–49
    genetic counseling for,
        23, 67–69
Parham case, 80–81
Pennhurst case, 81
Pennhurst State School and
    Hospital, 81–82
Phenothiazine, 61
Physical disabilities, 37
Physical therapy, 63, *64-65*
Physicians, 78–80
Pica, 58
Pineland Decree, 77–78

Prenatal diagnosis, 69–72,
    71
Prevention of mental
    retardation, 67–72, 79
Psychotherapy, 62–63
Public Law, 94–142, 30,
    38

Recessive genes, 18, 19,
    70
Rehabilitation Act, 42
Research about mental
    retardation, 72–76
Residential schools and
    institutions. *See*
    Institutionalization
Resource Room, 38
Rights of mentally retarded
    people, 77–83
Romeo, Nicholas, 81–82
Rubella, 24

Séguin, Edward O., 26–28, 62
Self-help skills, 50, 63–66
Senate, U.S., *54*
Severe mental retardation,
    36
Sexually transmitted
    diseases, 24–25
Siblings, 13–15
Simon, Theodore, 31
Socially appropriate
    behavior, 47, 60
Special education,
    mainstreaming vs., 37–40, *39*

Spina bifida, 20
Stanford-Binet Intelligence
    Test, 33, 51
Sterilization, 79
Supreme Court, U.S., 77,
    80–81, 82
Syphilis, 25

Tardive dyskinesia, 61
Terman, Lewis M., 33
Toileting, 36, 63–66
Training. *See* Education
    and training
Trisomy, 21,
Trumbull, H. Rutherford,
    III, 81
Tuberculosis (TB), 59

Victor (wild boy), 26, *27*
Vocational training and
    placement, 42, 50–53,
    52
Von Recklinghausen's
    disease, 18

Wayne County Training
    School, 51
Wechsler, David, 33
Wheat, Mary J., 81
World War II, 51

X-linked recessive
    disorders, 19, 70